*Was Going So Well…,
Then We Found Jesus*

How Christianity Deceived The Black Nation

Published by
Secretarius MEMPS Ministries

*Everything Was Going So Well...,
Then We Found Jesus*

HOW CHRISTIANITY DECEIVED THE BLACK NATION

By
Elijah Muhammad
(Messenger of Allah)
Minister Nasir Makr Hakim
(Editor)

~ ~ ~ ~ ~

Published by
Secretarius MEMPS Ministries
12685 Dorsett Rd #187 • Maryland Hts., MO 63043
Phone and Fax (314) 564-4003
http://www.memps.com

Copyright © 2006
Secretarius MEMPS Ministries

All rights reserved.
No part of this book may be reproduced
in any form, except for the inclusion of
brief quotations in reviews, without
permission in writing from the
author/publisher.

ISBN# 1-884855-61-X

Printed in the United States of America

Everything Was Going So Well, Then We Found Jesus

TABLE OF CONTENT

TABLE OF CONTENT..IV

DEDICATION.. V

INTRODUCTION VII

CHRISTIANITY DECEIVED THE BLACK NATION 1

TRUTH UPSETS CHRISTIAN WORLD............................ 15

WHITE AMERICA IS ANGRY BECAUSE OF THE TRUTH 25

NO JUSTICE FOR BLACK PEOPLE UNDER RULE OF WHITE PEOPLE... 39

OUR ENEMIES SEEK TO DESTROY US 53

NEGRO PREACHER WORSE ENEMY TO HIS PEOPLE... 63

GIVE UP THAT OLD SLAVERY IDEA 81

TRUE RELIGION.. 97

ACCEPT YOUR OWN AND BE YOURSELF 113

DEDICATION

To all the Believers and Followers
of
Elijah Muhammad,
Messenger of Allah,
without whom, we as fractions
would have no expectation
of ever becoming whole.

~ ~ ~ ~ ~

The
Messenger
is a Sword
In A Man's Hand.
~ *Sayings of Elijah Muhammad, Vol. 3*

Everything Was Going So Well, Then We Found Jesus

INTRODUCTION

If you want to talk to Allah, read the Holy Qur'an. If you are my followers, then seek the way through me. In fact, belief in me is sufficient.

The implication of these statements made by Elijah Muhammad, Messenger of Allah, are quite profound to say the least. What they mean to you and me is immeasurable.

In past histories, God has guided the course of things through prophets, messengers and the like; however, communication with them has primarily been through inspiration, visions and dreams. The foreknowing of God has been illustrated in the scriptures these representatives of God brought. It pointed out what a given people were going to do after the appearance of the respective messenger as well as how they would act after he was gone. In the scripture they brought or/and revealed, they spoke of another one coming after them, because they all were forerunners of a "Last One" who would actually be with God in the end. Although many of their utterances entailed the before-mentioned as well as that which would lead up to the appearance of the last one with God, where in the scriptures do we find what would take place after God's initial visit? We are in that time now.

In the past after prophets and messenger made their appearance and passed on, their record was left to the people to whom they had gone or from whom they were raised. The results are on the pages of history and have taken the forms of complete rejection of what was brought to the extreme of total misrepresentation.

There is either secularism – a total rejection of spirituality - to the extreme of believing that everything is god with an interpret-as-you-go attitude.

All of this makes the case for why God Himself has to come to make this crooked way straight. As the Bible and Holy Qur'an points out, this is exactly why the last messenger is with God in the end. His job is to serve as an example of how we are to interact with God, especially after being taught the reality of God. Once this Last One teaches what God truly is and our relationship to Him, we must be re-educated in how to act accordingly. When it comes to obedience, faith, love, service, success, etc..., this last one is to be the physical and spiritual example for us.

Fulfilling this mission means telling us the truth regardless of the price. The enemy of truth has killed the very prophets and messengers of God in the past; what makes us think he has changed? He knows his time is up and he intends to fight to the very end. Consequently, to get that truth to you, somebody had to pay a price or wager their own lives in exchange for that delivery.

EVERYTHING WAS GOING SO WELL, THEN WE FOUND JESUS

The Bible talks about a redemption. What is that? Have you ever redeemed soda bottles or milk bottles? When you returned the property of another, you were compensated, right? The so-called Negroes belong to the white man, because they were made property and are presently without the knowledge of who they are. They do not naturally belong to the white man, but possession is 9/10ths ownership according to the law. Allah does not come and forcibly take the so-called Negroes back, but once you are exposed to the truth of who you really are, you can willfully "return to your own" or "reclaim your own." You can see why exposing you to truth will "set you free." Yet, the truth bearer is the number one enemy of those who hide the truth. He has killed all he could in the past; therefore, if one decides to assume the role of telling you the truth or exposing you to truth, that one does so at the risk of their lives. This is the price for telling the truth.

When God came and began telling us the truth and waking us up, he was arrested (they didn't know He was God; for He came without observation), and when they questioned Him, He said, *"My name is W. F. Muhammad. I came to North America by myself..."* Yet, every time this happened, He sent for Elijah Muhammad to show him what the price would be if he took on this mission. The fact that Messenger Muhammad lived through it all and never altered that message for over 40 years is a worthy testimony that will be elaborated on in another upcoming book titled, <u>I Call Him Faithful</u>.

This book, however, addresses how Christianity deceived the black nation and when the truth of this deception is made known, it will upset the Christian world. A deceiver, especially one who is deemed the "arch" deceiver, is expected to go beyond mere upset. An arch-deceiver's primary existence rests on being hidden or unexposed. When light is shed on such a one, it is equal to death; consequently, this is why the world is angry, especially America. He is known to have never given her once-slave justice in her courts or anywhere else. Her mistreatment of the slave is world renown. In fact, no black people on the planet have been given any justice under white rule.

The white man is not what we think he is. We have been deceived alright; however, we think it is simply him having more power than us or withholding certain knowledge. This is partly the case. What we don't know is that he is a natural enemy. In other words, he is made for that purpose. He cannot help himself; this is one reason his warlike and murderous nature is consistent regardless of geography or time. As a natural predator, he continually seeks to destroy us.

Among his prey in America and elsewhere, he makes preachers to preach his religion; a religion that is made for the sole purpose of enslaving black people. This makes the preacher of Christianity willing agents of death to black people. This religion paralyses the mind and renders the adherer spiritually dead; and as a man or woman thinketh, so are they. We need to give up that old slavery way of thinking.

True "religion" is revealed to us once again, which was made in the beginning time when God created Himself. When the house was originally made, the original rules were made. All of this was made by the Original man. Now that we are blessed to have this knowledge revealed to us once again, we must accept our own and be ourselves.

Many may have lost hope or think that those in power will forever stay in power. This is how the disbelievers and hypocrites believed just before God destroyed them. We must believe that God has come to restore all things and who are in need of restoring more than we, the American so-called Negroes? He makes all things new!

The reader will find these aspects fully cover in this book. It is a compilation of the following radio broadcasts by Elijah Muhammad Messenger of Allah, and can be secured with a donation from Secretarius MEMPS Ministries: RB037, RB027, RB015, RB036, RB024, RB025, RB046, RB040, & RB041.

Thank you for your support of this ministry.

As-Salaam-Alaikum (Peace Be Unto You)

Nasir Makr Hakim
Minister of Elijah Muhammad, Messenger of Allah

How Christianity Deceived The Black Nation

EVERYTHING WAS GOING SO WELL, THEN WE FOUND JESUS

CHRISTIANITY DECEIVED THE BLACK NATION

Greetings to you; I am Elijah Muhammad, the preacher of freedom, justice, and equality to my people, the American Black man and woman, who have been lost from our people for the last 400 or more years. We are no more a lost people, but are now found. We have been found by God Himself, as the prophets predicted we would. Behold He cometh without observation, but blessed is he who believe in Him the same shall become the sons of God.

We do not need to look for the coming of God. We do not need to be on our knees praying and thinking that God will come out of the sky like some spook or some formless thing. Today, we have God in Person with us, to whom praises are due forever, in the person of Master Fard Muhammad. He came in the person of a man. He is not coming in the way we have been thinking in the past: that God would come to us as a spirit; no, my beloved readers, my people. God is a man and not a spook. Spooks have no joy or interest in any material things, not to think over the affairs of you and me. He said that we are from the Tribe of Shabazz, who has been here in the Western Hemisphere for the last 400 years.

We are referred to as Negroes. This is only a slang name given to us by our slave masters when we were babies. After being spoiled and robbed of the knowledge of self and others, the slave masters gave us this name, which means something that is neutral, lifeless, dead and have to be moved or carried wherever one wants it to be. According to what Almighty God, Allah, said to me, the lost and found members of the great Asiatic Nation, the Black Nation, the original people of the earth, the first and last, if there ever is to be a last, has no birth record.

We must forget the fairy tales taught to us by our slave master's children through Christianity. Forget about that religion altogether. It is not the religion that you should be believing in today. This is a religion that was formed by the Caucasian race for the purpose of deceiving the black people of the world and they did just that. Our fathers suffered 300 years in servitude slavery and we had no spiritual teacher of truth to teach us anything that would deliver us from the chains of ignorance and physically slavery to the white race. Not only were we without here in America, but around the earth.

The white race has ruled the black people of the earth with a very, very heavy and torturous and unmerciful hand, having no mercy whatsoever in ruling the Black man. He ruled over the black man without any mercy. He rules the black man with death. He rules the black nations with fear and finally, slavery and death. Today we must remember that we no more are in the ignorance of yesterday; we have the truth today. We know this people. Almighty God Allah, to whom praise is due forever, has appeared in the person of Master Fard Muhammad, and has revealed the truth to us. Also, He has opened our eyes to reality and not to foolishness. He has not opened our eyes to sport and play, but has opened them to the reality of truth and the internalizing of wisdom like men. He has introduced us to the practice of truth and the practice of that which brings to us the good things that we thought would come to us after death, which was taught by the slavery teachings of Christianity. This teaching cannot ever be accepted. It is not the teachings of truth; it's a teaching other than truth. It makes us or forces us to believe in that which will never bring salvation, freedom, justice and equality to us. It teaches a servitude spiritual slavery. It binds the spiritual thinking of you and me into slavery thinking and a belief in that which will never bring to us anything but slavery and death. We hear s lot of this going on now, but let us take a look at the Christians themselves.

The Christian nation of Europe and America or where ever they may be on the earth, cannot help themselves today. Today, there is no power in the religion of Christianity to save Europe, America and the world of Christianity, from the chastisement and doom of Almighty God Allah. There is no hope for them in Christianity. There is no power in Christianity to deliver us from the great destruction of the nations of the earth today. The world of Christianity today is sitting on a powder keg, as it is referred to. Not only is it sitting on a powder keg that is well sealed so they won't go off, but the fuse has been lit and the explosion can take place at any moment, because the time has arrived when truth and justice must destroy falsehood and injustice. The American leadership of my people, the black people is deceived, greatly deceived. They are gravely deceived in that which they have been accepting as truth. They are deceived into thinking that one day they will rise up as spirits out of the cemeteries. They are deceived into looking forward to seeing spirits as angels coming in the clouds of the heaven. I'm sorry, but they won't be invisible. Those angels are visible people sent by God to destroy the world. When you see them, there will be no joy for you who disbelieve; so says the Holy Qur'an.

You have rejected the real truth of Almighty God for the last 35 years. You have rejected God Himself, as it is written that you would do. Now the day of judgment is before us. We are living in the days of judgment. We are living in days of Allah, God Almighty, whose day it is to rule. It is His time; it is His Sabbath, it is the time that you and me should rise up and lay hold to the truth and guidance of our God. It is the day and time when every man will taste that which he has done of good or evil; this is the time. It is only God Almighty Himself, in the person of Master Fard Muhammad, Who can forgive us and pass over our sins, as it is written. God comes and seeketh to save that which was lost;

save it from what? He will save it from the destruction of His enemies. It is the so called Negroes, who are really not Negroes, but the lost and found members of their great Aboriginal Nation, who God comes and searches for. It is their sins that will be forgiven if they will submit to the will of Almighty God, Allah, obey Him and follow His chosen messenger. It is the doom of any people, according to the history of the past, who will, after the knowledge of the truth, willfully ignore the truth and follow the falsehood of that people whose life is doomed for total destruction. It was so with the people of Noah. It was so with the people of Lot. It was so with the people of Moses, Pharaoh and his people. There was a judgment set between Moses' people and Pharaoh that is made so clear as a sign for you and me here today. We are under a hard master; a master unwilling to give justice to us, a master who is unwilling to even let you go free for ourselves to do something for ourselves. This you know, whether you will bear me witness or not.

Everything Was Going So Well, Then We Found Jesus

The so-called American Negroes are a hundred years up from slavery. The slave master's children say they (meaning the Negroes) are free, yet are not willing to give them justice in their courts. Not willing to provide them with something to go for themselves, he holds them here as a prey. This is true and is clear as sunshine. The white man holds the Negro as a prey. Produce a way for him to lead. "No, we don't want him to lead." He's fighting the freedom of the Negro all the time. He opposes the Negro in getting equal justice in their courts. We are justly due some of America; for our fathers as well as ourselves have spent our lives here enriching the white race with everything that they bid us to help them in for 400 years. In going forth early in the morning and coming in late in the evening, we worked hard all day for 400 years to help make America the Garden of Eden, the paradise for the white man. He is living in good homes throughout the country - some of them are over a million or two dollars, (the value of them. All of this wealth invested in the beautiful homes of white people and it was the poor old slave who have prepared these beautiful homes with his sweat and blood. The Continental of America is now criss-cross with some of the finest railroads and some of the finest road and stock iron that the world ever seen. She's rich with those spikes that pin the steel down to those ties of wood driven by the poor black man with his sweat dropping off from his brow on those spikes hit and the spike hammer. What has he gotten for this? What has he been offered other than being chased by his enemies from one state to another? After he has made this great sacrifice with his life for his master, today the master doesn't want to even give him equal justice. Human rights he doesn't enjoy; civil rights he doesn't enjoy. He doesn't enjoy any rights, but the right to be a subject to his white slave masters. This he has come to love, because of a few dollars paid to him for work. He then takes it and spends it for whiskey, beer, ball games, and sports of all kind. He wastes his earned money. He won't even take a nickel out of every day's work and put it up or bank it for himself. I have appealed to you for years to let us all sacrifice one nickel a day - 22 million people - and see what you will have in a black bank of your own at the end of the year. Would you do that? *"No, because you (Elijah) are a black man and I don't want a black man handling my money. I want my slave master's children who robbed me of everything to continue to rob me, to hold my money for me."*

My friend you are in a bad way of thinking. You are in a bad way of relying upon the enemy who has destroyed you. I have asked you to let us ask America for a territory to ourselves here. We have well earned it. We need a few states to ourselves. Separate us, since they only want us for free slave purposes. They only want us in a position where they can keep us under perfect control with the police's night stick, his gun and with the state troopers rifles and tear gas. They want you like that; they don't want you living across the line in another state, though it may join their state. They want the so-called American Negro under the gun, under their power where they can treat them as they please and that's with a beating, death and with a few dollars for their labor. I want to warn you while on that subject. A few dollars are becoming so worthless until one day you will soon wake up and find that America's dollar that you rob and kill each other for, will not even be worth taking out in a waste basket and throwing it into the furnace. These things are bound to come upon you in few days, as God Almighty has said, through the mouth of His prophets and has made it clear to me out of His mouth. He said that America's money will not be worth any more than discarded newspapers. The day is now approaching and I want to say to you my beloved brothers and sisters who are reading this book, you're living in the day of the judgment of America. God has said He would judge America first.

We are in the day of the anger of the nations of the earth. This is the day when peace won't be accepted from where you and I live – America. The nations of the earth don't want any peace with America and if the nations of the earth don't want any peace with America, I say brothers and sisters, old slave, once slave, ex slave, what should he do? He should fly for his life. This is no time for you to be planning on sport, play and chasing each other all over the country to see which one can be the leader. You can't be a leader today unless it's in the grave of ignorance and hell fire. You cannot be that which you are not made for. The leader of this people today must be a leader of whom God Himself chooses; you can't lead yourself, so how can you lead others except in the way that Jesus prophesied that you would lead: the blind leading the blind and they both fall in the ditch together. I want you to remember that ditch is hell, not a place of enjoyment. You will catch hell today trying to lead against the wishes of Almighty God Allah. For the man who noweth not God, His purpose and His aims for the nations of the earth today, you are one who is blind, deaf, and dumb spiritually and should not seek to lead others in the condition that you're in, but you should seek the spiritual light of that one whom God Himself has raise up among you I and guides him to guide you, has his power, and his protection for him and those who follow him. This is the man that you should seek and I'm just that man.

You can believe it or not. You are in trouble and don't know it. I beg you to listen to the truth. I try to persuade you to listen to the truth and follow after the truth. Every nation today is angry, as it is written in your own Bible, that at that time, the nations would be angry. In the 11th chapter and the 18th verse of Revelations; turn your pages over and read it, *"And the nations were angry and thy wrath has come, the time of the dead that they should be judged."* This is referring to you and me. We are the dead to whom justice should come. We are the dead that should be raise up and given an equal chance as other nations. The nations are angry. God is angry. The Messenger is angry. The righteous are angry. There's not even one percent (1%) satisfied. Every man of all the nations of the earth today is dissatisfied. One Hundred percent (100%) dissatisfaction exists over the nations of the earth today.

TRUTH UPSETS CHRISTIAN WORLD

Today, there is much confusion and controversy surrounding the teaching of God's presence, the religion of Islam and the doom of the race of the white man. The coming of God, the judgment of the world, and the resurrection of the dead seems to have caused more upset, stirring and confusions of the nation than all the preaching of the church for hundreds of years. All my life I have seen preachers storming the churches with such sermons of hellfire, the rise of the dead and the going to heaven of one party and the other party to hell. The people use to sit and listen to these preachers and became exited and fearful. The Bible and Holy Qur'an is full of the teachings of the resurrection of the dead, how it will take place and how it will end, one party being saved and one party being doomed to total destruction. Yet, when the same teaching is mentioned or preached today by the Muslims, it seems to cause more excitement and confusion to rise, even though such teaching is clearer today than ever before.

Today we are charged with sedition, seeking the overthrow of the government and destruction of the white race, for preaching the upcoming judgment of the world; when in fact, I simply would like to make more clearer the understandings of the message given to me by Almighty God Allah, the truth of it, the time we are living in and what we should expect in this time if we believe in the prophets and their predictions of this time. If we don't believe in the prophets, we don't believe in God. If we won't believe in the prophets' messages they brought to us, namely the scriptures (Bible and Holy Quran), we won't believe in the sender of these messengers.

These are very trying days. These are very evil days. These are very deceitful days. These are very murderous, bloody days of the nations. These are the days of trouble. These are the days of wide spread evils. These are the days of calamities and continuous destructions of lives and property of people and nations. And these are the days of the resurrection of the dead that have been talked about so much and its coming prophesied to us. These are the days that we are now living in.

I give praise and thanks to Allah for His coming in these days and time in which we are living and for bringing to us the truth that had been hidden from the hearts, ears and eyes of the people for a very long time; since the creation of Adam or the creation of the white race.

The creation of Adam refers to the creation of the white race. Today, this truth of that race, their creation, their rule, their ending, the rule of the black man and his absence in ruling, is all to be made clear and understandable. This truth was sealed until the end of the Caucasian's civilization

Being so dead to the knowledge of truth, referring to my people, it is something strange to them to hear the name of another religion and the name of a God that the slave master and his children never taught them to believe in or accept. Exposing this truth, the truth of the white race, the truth of the black nation, the truth of everything that had been hidden from us, has now upset the white race to such a degree that they are going here and there trying to get the understanding of just why that this truth is now bursting forth in the West as never before. They see the truth as something that is going to interfere with their success and continued rule over the black man of the earth and something that will prevent them from keeping the so-called American Negro forever down helpless under their feet of civilization.

How Christianity Deceived The Black Nation

Today, we find them doing everything possible to make it appear that what I am teaching is from myself and not from God; but from myself. They try to make it appear that I have went and planned all of this, wrote it on paper and am teaching our people something I have thought up. I'm not able to think up no such wisdom alone. I was too dumb to think into such a deep wisdom. It is from God Whose proper name is Allah, Who appeared in the person of Master Fard Muhammad.

Another aspect they seems to be confused over is the coming of God in the person of a man; yet, they preached that God came in the person of Jesus and he was a man in every respect when he was born and when he died. He was nothing but a human being; however, they thinks it is absolutely false to teach that God is a man when in fact the Bible they preach from and from what they say Jesus said when he was here, prophesied the coming of the Son of Man, not the coming of a spirit or a spook, but the coming of the Son of Man to usher in the judgment of the world. They teach that Jesus said, as well as their Bible teaches, that this Son of Man would be the Judge on the day of judgement. This is so clear that it needs no interpretation; for they declared that He will be the Son of a Man, not a son of a spirit or spook as the church or the ignorant preachers of the church who have not understood the scriptures, desire you to believe. They don't believe that God is human. They believe or say that if He's human he died like we. The President or the Kings are human beings and they come and go. They die, nevertheless another one comes and takes the seat immediately behind him. He also is called the same or has the same honor as his predecessor.

So it is with God; the Bible teaches the coming of God and if God has to come it is definitely a proof that he was not already here, because He had to come. When He comes, He would give life to the dead, destroy the wicked, their kingdom, their civilization and all that goes for it and set up a kingdom of righteousness, a kingdom of peace. What type of people would He choose or what type of people would be His choice? According to the Bible and according to the Holy Quran, He will choose the people that civilization had rejected and despised as a member, equal member of their society; this is the so-called American Negroes who are also considered a foolish people: A people who has no sense; this is the so-called American Negroes, a people who loves and worship devils; this is the so called American Negroes, a people who has no knowledge of self and others; this is the American so-called Negroes, of whom the Bible and Holy Quran calls the spiritually dead, deaf, dumb and blind. They are spiritually blind, because they cannot see and distinguish truth from falsehood. This is the people that God would choose for His elect nation; He will choose them. He will call them after His own name. He will strip them, according to Isaiah, of their old names of Satan and the Bible's Revelations makes mention of the same: that He will call them after His own Holy names. These things are now being fulfilled right in the eyes of the people who read and preach this Gospel; yet, they are blind to the knowledge of its fulfillment, or the manifestation that is right now in their face. We are the people, the American so-called Negroes, whom God now chooses to be His people to build the Kingdom of righteousness, freedom, justice and equality as practitioners and examples of purity of faith in Him.

The American so-called Negroes were the first to recognize Him. It is this people from whom God will choose the Last Messenger. It is this people from whom He has already chosen the Last Messenger. Like this people, the Bible says, His messenger would also be blind deaf and dumb as any of the others and among them it is prophesied would be his work, power and authority.

We even find it there in the Revelation of the Bible that he's referred to as being the First

Begotten of the Dead. Preachers have preached this all their lives and represent it to be referring to the death and rise of Jesus; however, there has been no physical resurrection of Jesus since he was killed 2,000 years ago in Jerusalem. No. There could not be no such prophesy of God, or as one the people calls the Son of God, being the first from the dead, because this means the mentally dead. The resurrection means the rise of those who were blind, deaf and dumb to the knowledge of truth; therefore, God could not be referred to as one coming into the resurrection or being resurrected among the dead when He is the power of the resurrection. He is the one Who causes the resurrection and gives the dead power to rise; so, how can He be referred to as being the first begotten of the dead? This is looking at the physical side of the matter, when actually the text refers to the spiritual resurrection of the dead and not a physical resurrection. I am the first begotten of the dead. It is like someone saying I am the first that He risen up in this part of the world, which is just like saying that.

Everything Was Going So Well, Then We Found Jesus

The truth is becoming so strong in the West that it is absolutely has the West bewildered. The people are running to and fro trying to find something to disprove the truth, but the more that they seek to disprove it, the brighter the truth becomes.

WHITE AMERICA IS ANGRY BECAUSE OF THE TRUTH

We are suffering due to the lack of justice, the lack of recognition as human beings, and the lack of the knowledge of ourselves, which is the result of being robbed by our slave masters. Our enemies brought us here from our original people, from our native land and country, for the purpose of making us to bear a burden for them.

We have given them slave labor for the past 400 years. For the first three hundred years we have been in servitude slavery and the remaining one hundred years, we have been free slaves.

I want to say to you my beloved brothers and sisters of the original Black Nation of the earth, the first and the last, the father of the creation of the heavens and the earth, as Almighty God, Allah, has taught me, that we, the Black Nation here in America, are the original people and are now living in the time that we must return to our own or be removed as a people from the earth.

This is the teaching of Almighty God, Allah, Who came in the person of Master Fard Muhammad, in 1930, to whom be praises forever. We should teach our children to praise Him forever and their children should teach their children. We should forever give praise and thanks to God for having mercy on us and coming to our rescue by bringing us the light of truth so that we may be able to walk in the right path and know each other and love each other as brothers and sisters, which we were created and made to do. He came to restore the love that our enemies robbed us of. He came to unite us, because our enemies have divided, spoiled and robbed us of the knowledge of self, which is the worst and greatest robbery of all robberies.

He couldn't be robbed any worst. For it is worst than robbing him of all his earthly wealth and depriving him even of freedom, but to then go and rob him of the knowledge of self, is a grave crime. He could go to jail, he could stay there with a head full of wisdom, but to go and rob him of the knowledge of self, he has already jailed him and has imprisoned him in the worst prison house that he could be imprisoned in, which is one that is without the knowledge of self.

It is a shame to see how some of our educators acts. To listen to them talk, makes us shame. Not having the knowledge of self after getting diplomas and degrees from the white man's colleges and universities, makes us feel bad for them after hearing them. This is terrible.

Let us give praise and thanks to Master Fard Muhammad, Almighty God in person; forever we shall praise Him. We shall pray to Him for what we want and He shall give it to us. For 33 years

I know these things to be true, whatever I asked Him in prayer he has granted. I fear not that He will not answer a believer's prayer, I know He will. I have tried Him in answering prayers and he has always answered me. I never ask for anything that is of vanity. I never have asked for that which I didn't need or want to see come to pass of good. I never did asked him for anything to tempt Him; no. He's not to be tempted. He's self independent and He has no need for anything. He doesn't need to prove Himself by our tempting Him. He's self sufficient, and self independent. He don't need us, but we need's Him. All praise is due to Allah in the person of Master Fard Muhammad and peace be upon the prophets of Allah and His mercy and His blessings: Noah, Abraham, Moses, Jesus and Muhammad, peace be on them - old prophets of Allah.

Now, we come to the time of the manifestation of the truth. We must face facts and not forget that we must face actual facts today. The coming of God is for that purpose of making the truth known and to bring out that which is hidden of the truth or make it manifest. It makes the evil that is hidden to the eye of man, manifest. He's the Manifester and today we have no need to fear and flinch from truth, because it is here. He's like a Sun in the morning, which brightens the shadow of the earth and reveals that which was hidden last night from our eyes, and in the sunlight, we see it all clearly as it is; so it is today with the nations, people, language and towns. Everything is to be made manifest, America is included.

America is the first, according to the teachings or the word of Almighty God to me, to be made manifest as the evilest of all the people of the earth. She has robbed and spoiled a whole nation, the black man, by bringing them here 400 years ago for the purpose of robbing him and for the purpose of enslaving him and making him do all of her labor, and taking part in fighting her enemies; yet, she herself being his main enemy. She kills her slave and deprives her once slave of freedom, justice and equality day and night while some of us lie down at her feet waddling on the floor, in the sand, in the dust, and in the mud begging and crying while his heavy foot is kicking and stamping all throughout this begging and moaning for justice. Yet, with all of this, white America, God is not sleep. He was bound to repay you for it and the time has arrived.

Allah, Who appeared in the person of Master Fard Muhammad, has come after this people. He intends not to be defeated. He has never lost a battle and never will loose one. It is a sin and a disgrace to see the poor American so-called Negroes in such a pitiful condition in America without the knowledge of self and begging all over the country for justice, for an equal chance, for freedom indeed and seeking to join on to those of his enemy who brought him into subjection. He has gone astray and lost the knowledge of himself and he's absolutely like a physical blind man going around walking through the streets grabbing and feeling for anything that feel like something that he can stand by.

It is pitiful, it is pitiful. The cry of our people day and night goes up into the ears of God from the lash and the night sticks of the vicious police department who has been permitted by the government to use their clubs freely on Negroes' heads and their guns with hot bullets running through his body. This is going on throughout the country day and night, 24 hours a day. The poor so-called American Negro suffers at the hands of the white man. The very looks of some of the white people, especially in the South, at the so-called American Negro is enough to put him to swimming across the Atlantic or the Pacific back to Asia from wince he came. It is a very pitiful sight.

Everything Was Going So Well, Then We Found Jesus

In 1959 I talked to scholars in the Islamic world who sit and cried with tears in their eyes over the evil and suffering condition of us in America under the white man. They all know, however, as we too now know, it's only a matter of time that Almighty God Allah will show Himself as He did in Ancient times when a government or people exceeded all good. He did so in the days of Lot; He did so in the days of Noah; He did so at the Red Sea in the day of Moses and now all of these histories and examples of Almighty God Allah's work serves as no warning at all to the wicked brute forces of America, because Allah has revealed them to be none other than the devils themselves, which is why they are angry. The truth of them has been revealed and they now seek to destroy we to whom Allah has brought the truth. They are not able to attack Him; so, they seek to take revenge on us who believe, as it is written, because they hate the truth. They hate the God of truth and of justice, as it written again in the Bible, in the Revelation. They know wrath is coming, and also the wrath of God is coming. It is time for God to get angry.

Look how His righteous people are being treated under a government and people as the Caucasian people. They have ever mistreated the Muslims. They have ever hated Allah and Islam. They never wanted Islam to cross the Atlantic and the Pacific to get into the ears of the so-called American Negro. This is one religion they even kept in secret among themselves to talk of. We hardly ever remember hearing them use the word Islam or Allah.

They have ever tried to keep this religion, the prophets religion, which is divine supreme being's religion or entire submission to the Will of Almighty God, Allah from the American so-called Negroes. No man could be a believer in God unless he was a believer in Islam, because without entire submission to the Will of God, we cannot be His servants. That is the best and only religion God ever had from the days He created the universe.

EVERYTHING WAS GOING SO WELL, THEN WE FOUND JESUS

My beloved readers, I preach separation of our people. Many of our people think it's really a mockery, a shame and a crime even as much as to preach that we should be separated from the white people - a people who has never given us justice and who's parents and grandparents beat and lashed our poor grandparents, great grandparents and great grandparents for many, many years. For centuries, our poor people fell under the lash, and have been lynched, burned on the soil of America time and again, and today a ready policeman stands with his club and an itching finger to shoot, beat and kill a black so-called Negro if he just makes the least act of disorder. If the poor so-called Negro provoke him to anger in the least bit, that's a dead man and in the courts it would be deemed justified for killing the so-called American Negro. They always justify killing the poor, 400 year old, innocent Negro, who still suffers without any justice, without any chance of justice, under the law and banner of the American government.

Take for instance Mr. Duffy, the federal court judge in Chicago. According to the Chicago Tribune newspaper, making his remarks of hatred for we the Muslims, my followers and myself, that we were not even entitled to justice under the constitution as far as religion is concerned, because we were not a religious people or we weren't teaching religion. We were only racists and should not be given any justice under the constitution's laws.

This is very terrible and very evil; especially, after our parents have slaved their lives out for Judge Duffy's parents and himself then, now today he openly says to we who has turned from evil and are trying to do good, that the government should not give any justice to us and classify us as enemies trying to overthrow the white race; yet, we are not trying to overthrow the white race, but rather trying to overthrow falsehood that has come into the ears of our people and trying to replace falsehood with truth that Almighty God Allah has given to us. If truth will overthrow the white race, judge Duffy, I say your race is gone, because we must have truth today regardless to the dislike of you or the whole entire Caucasian race. We must have the truth. It is time for the truth. It is time for the presence of God. It is time for the deliverance and separation of the poor old black people whom you have beaten and killed for many centuries. It is time that they should go from you, but you are angry, because it is time and you desire to keep them for no other purpose than to mistreat them. You don't intend to give the Christian believing Negro justice; in fact, you are not doing it. All of those who worship your religion and you in the church, bowing to you and waddling themselves on the ground for justice, you're not giving them any, not to think of we the Muslims. Of course, every Muslim that believes in Allah and believes that I am His messenger, they don't have to waddle at the feet of no nation. God is sufficient; Allah is sufficient to give us what we want. He's sufficient to give us justice. He's sufficient to defend us and we rely on Him alone.

Judge Duffy and the haters of the Muslims wish to see the Muslims deprived of everything that goes for justice, because of their hatred of truth. I cannot blame them. I cannot say that they shouldn't do these things, because judge Duffy and his whole race, as God have said, were created to be enemies of the truth and enemies of justice; therefore, there is no justice for us in America. No black, so-called Negro, whether he's Muslim, Buddhist, Jewish, or a Christian believer, it don't make any difference, there's no justice for a so-called Negro in America.

The filthy social equality that is being offered to him and the opportunity to marry his lower class white people, is only a ploy allowing him into the worst of his people to then get him to hate his own people and hate the salvation that is waiting for him. This is what this is all for. I preach separation, and the only way we will ever enjoy freedom, justice and equality it is to be separated from our enemies and go on some of this earth that we can call our own. Allah will help us to get some of it. We won't beg an enemy of ours to give it to us, we will beg Allah for it and Allah is well able to give us some of this earth wherever we desire to have it. As it is written by the prophets and declared in the Holy Qur'an, He will give it to us if we obey and do His will. He will give us whatever we ask for. He will delight in doing so.

I teach separation and believe in it. I believe in the separation of schools. If we ever expect to rear our children up in a decent life as God fearing, clean minded children, we had better put them in a school to themselves and teach them our ourselves, because the public schools of the enemy destroys the morals of black children regardless of what school you enter. With them, your child is gone in the way of hell.

NO JUSTICE FOR BLACK PEOPLE UNDER RULE OF WHITE PEOPLE

I seek justice, freedom and equality for you. I am seeking a home on this earth that you can call your own; a home wherein you can live in peace to yourselves; a home wherein you will have no fear of enemies invading it while you're awake or while you're asleep; a home that you will not fear being bombed or waylaid to come out of your house to be shot down; a home where these things will not exist; a home wherein you can be proud of yourselves with brotherhood among your own enjoying the peace and friendship of all civilized people of the world. Allah will set you in heaven at once, which is money, good homes, and friendship in all walks of life. This is for you who will submit to Allah, the Almighty God, Who has perfect control over the powers of the heavens, the earth and all the treasures therein. They belong to Him.

The great things that are now happening demand that you come closer together on the right way. You should know what to expect in these times. Being blind to the time in which you live and what you may expect in such times is death. It is like living under death, because you are subject to death. This is addressed to those who have not the knowledge of the time, because you will make no preparation for what will happen in the time. It is you my people who I call on, because you have been lost from your own kind for the past 400 years; however, you have been found by God Himself, and He now calls on you and me to make ready ourselves to unite onto our own kind and accept our own. This is being asked of you and me to accept our own.

One of the greatest and the noblest subject or text that could be preached among us is to accept our own. Knowledge of your own is now being made crystal clear to you, because your own is not what you have been or still are thinking is.

One of the gravest mistakes you are making is ignorantly thinking that you should first unite with white people or intermix with them before ever finding a way of uniting with the people of whom you are a member; the people from whom you were brought. You should be eager and intelligent enough to first get in unity with your own people before trying seeking unity and love with our enemies who brought your fathers and my fathers into subjection and servitude slavery. They have mistreated them worse than any human being has ever been treated since there were men on the face of the earth.

The white race has mistreated us so terribly bad that there is no equal or any comparison for it. There is nothing you could compare to the type of suffering and evil inflicted on our fathers and ourselves - their children – by the hand of the white man. You and I have been and still are denied freedom, justice and equality - that you will agree.

It is outright foolish for you and me to go back to the same original source that deprived us of freedom, justice and equality, while at the same time attempting to shut out the truth from our ears by seeking to exile and kill those who try bringing us the truth. We are foolish to go to the white man seeking freedom, justice and equality from them, because they are the ones who have put us into the condition we are now in. They are the ones who killed and robbed our fathers of the knowledge of self, and we being their children are now actually was born blind, deaf and dumb from the cradle.

The white man even uses speeches made by so-called Negro leaders against the peace and future happiness of the poor black so-called Negroes in America and would like to use them to be their ambassador for control over the black man of Africa and Asia, but he has miserably failed.

Now, he could never go out of America as a peace maker in Africa for the African and the white man. Africa doesn't want him anymore on their soil; they have learned him. Africa is learning most all of the white loving so-called Negroes of America. They have their own men here as agents who are watching the American Negroes' ways and actions and the white man' actions towards the Negroes and are reporting it to their people in their respective government in Africa and in Asia hourly and daily. Why and for what purpose? Because a universal showdown is own it's way to rid the earth of trouble makers, haters of peace, lovers of war, lovers of spilling innocent blood, lovers of murder, and lovers of evil generally. It is on the way to a showdown; therefore, these things must be recorded to show justice for the executors of justice, that they are justified in the execution of the wicked. The righteous should be glad; for they have suffered under the hands of the wicked for 6,000 years.

This race of people has been created for the purpose of breaking the peace, making mischief in the land and causing bloodshed. It is the very nature of the white race to do such things. They are haters of righteousness; they don't love righteousness. They love evil, because their very nature is inclined to evil continuously.

They were made of such material or disposition, such as deceiving the righteous, making truth to appear as a lie and a lie appear as truth, breaking the general peace between the original man of the earth - the black man. They never have been able to live in peace themselves.

Of course, the law of consequences does not permit the peace breaker or the law breaker to continue without being punished; he must be punished. He must suffer the consequences of his own doing. This is the law of nature in which we cannot escape. We have to, as the old saying goes, "reap what we sow." This is justice. Make a man reap that which he sows or suffer the consequences of his own doings. This is nothing but right.

Here in America, the poor so-called Negro, were lost but are now found by God Almighty Himself, in the person of Master Fard Muhammad, to Whom praise is due forever. As long as there is a universe, His name shall be praised. The very name Muhammad means praise, worthy of praise and praise forever; this is one of God's names.

I say my beloved lost and found people, you are in a day of judgement of this evil race. The time has now approached into their windows and into their doors. The coming of God meant just that. It is not meant that He would leave the ruler of evil free to continue their rule; for two Gods cannot rule successfully the people of earth at the same time. The evil race called Caucasians or the white race, were given the knowledge by their evil God who is known throughout the history of the scripture or religious spiritual teaching of the prophets. The devils were made for the purpose of upsetting the peace of the people and that they should do this until they had been taken away. You have all of this in your Bible if you read it carefully, but you have not known who these people actually were. It is not that the black man is created evil, regardless of his evil actions and doings; he got that from the white man. All of that came from the white man, his evil doings. He's not really living his life; he's trying to live the life of the white race, not his own, but the white man's life. He's making a very great open failure of it. Even those trying to imitate the devils are hated by him and are miserably use by him and seeks to destroy them. This is the enemy; this is the real devil's purpose. They don't live in peace among themselves. They fight and war against one another and all of this is going on daily: fighting against one another. This is the world of sin; this is the world of evil whose God and judge is Satan himself; therefore, they have deceived the world and the black man is suffering the consequence of being ignorant to the knowledge of this race. He has made miserable mistakes that has caused him to fall victim at their murderous hands.

We must remember that we can't go to them seeking justice when they are the real destroyers of justice and haters of justice; as it was one Sunday in Flint, Michigan. We had no recourse there but to just walk out and give the city of Flint up to the authorities of Flint, who are wicked and haters of Black so-called Negroes and their desires for freedom justice and equality. We bowed out, because we do not have meetings; wherein, any police, detective, FBI or whatnot can stand armed in our service. This is only provoking and we are not for such. We don't go arm ourselves. We want to bring the world to its knees with the good and the power of God Almighty, Who is against arms. They use almighty arms for their defense, which is what the American white man or the white race in general depends on. They have hopes in their arms. God Almighty has said to me to carry no weapons. He said don't even allow my followers to carry weapons; not so much as a pin knife for the purpose of attacking the white man. He wants to show the American white man His power to defend we, the Muslims, who were lost and found and have no plants making arms for us, nor any access to arms whatsoever. Allah knows that we aren't equal in those kinds of weapons. He wants to show America that He has power over the arms, as it is written in Isaiah, that no weapons shall prosper against thee.

God has power over these things. We know, and I have seen God face to face and have received my mission directly from His mouth, as it is written that one would do. The last book of the prophets in the Bible teaches you that. The prophesy of Moses teaches you the same in that the last messenger would get his message directly from the mouth of God, not in a vision as the prophets who went before him, nor in a hidden manner as God gave it in the past as in being hidden in the bush; nor will it be by inspirations of righteousness from the righteous revealing things to them as to what they should best do. But today, God in person is with us and He directs me from Himself. Don't believe that I am insane in saying these things. The very work that I'm doing should testify to what I just said. It is the truth and it is proven that it is the truth. God has said to me not to carry any kind of weapon and that He wanted to fight Himself. In fact, He has told me that's exactly how it would come off and how we would be attacked, the time and number when He will come in and put a stop forever this evil wicked and beast like people, who hate Allah and Islam and the Muslim world. He would come in and take charge of the matter and settle it. I have all of this from Him; therefore, I don't want to make the grave mistake of trying to provoke His actions before time. I don't want to be charged with causing the death of the innocent by some foolish action or step that I would make;

therefore, we take it and suffer many embarrassing, shameful and evil actions made against us, because number one, our people are still dead to the knowledge of themselves and have no help coming to them. Number two, they are full of fear of the white man.

In a meeting October the 27th, in Flint Michigan, there we had rented a place to teach and had paid the full price thereof. There sat the enemies all around this place as though we were bank robbers or had come therw to rob the entire population of the Flint. There was an empty building directly across in front of the door of the place that we had rented filled with police so I am told. There they had binoculars on us looking at us across the street through the window and they were heavily armed. The house was full of heavily armed people and some of them were out of uniform. Most of them without uniform, disguised as just mere citizens, were ready to toss on us or start mowing us down from across the street. If they could have gotten us to provoke them by them sending and we keeping out their leader of the police force, the Captain, Commissioner or the Prosecuting attorney from coming in, they would have forced their way in and ignored our law of peace to come in just to break our law. This would have been nothing more than mischief making, as they are made to do by breaking up a peaceful assembly, breaking up a religious meeting held there for the purpose of making people more righteous and more peaceful. They came to break it up, because they don't want the Negroes to know the truth. They don't want the Negroes to be united and don't want the them to have friends; therefore, they do everything possible to make it appear as though we are absolute trouble makers and that they would have to be around us to keep us from starting trouble; even though in 32 years, which is our witness, we have never done a thing like making trouble. Yet, they come as they did in Los Angeles California, 1962, with the attack on Temple #27. After the trial, when the time came for sentencing the brothers there, they had buildings across in front of the courthouse, so I was told, that were very heavily armed with machine guns set up to mow the Muslims down.

This is the evilest and most deceptive people and countries that ever lived on our planet earth. What mercy should God show to a people like that? Even the very defenseless unarmed person cannot live in peace among them.

Well, I say remember the voice of Isaiah in the 59th chapter and the 14th verse: Judgment is turned away backwards from us and justice stands aside for truth is falling in the streets and equity cannot come in; it cannot enter. This is the world of Satan.

OUR ENEMIES SEEK TO DESTROY US

These original prophesies for the lost and found people of mine in the Western Hemisphere are very beautiful. The Bible and the Holy Qur'an are full of prophesies. They relate to the resurrection of the mentally dead of that lost and found people, their rising, and their opposition and victory over their great, mighty and open enemies.

The day has now come that Almighty God, Allah, desires to make Himself known as He did in the days of Moses and Pharaoh, when Moses went to Pharaoh to beg him to let Israel go, but Pharaoh and his people mistreated Israel. The Bible says that Pharaoh and his people put heavy burdens upon Israel to carry. They made Israel do two men's work for the same pay.

Everything Was Going So Well, Then We Found Jesus

This is the same for the American so called Negro. American not only deceives the Black Original Nation, but also physically mistreats and robs them of justice and their rights. This is going on at this very moment and is stepped up against the poor black man in the Western Hemisphere. There is no such thing as them wanting to give him justice. They don't have that in their nature. They just can't do these things that are not in their nature. I'm so sorry for you who continually beg them day and night for something which they have not been given by nature to give you. They cannot help but mistreat you. They were created for that purpose.

They speak about hate and charge Elijah with teaching hate. "You are teaching the black man to hate us." I want you to remember how this is being charged. He doesn't say that, "the such and such truth that Elijah is teaching is causing the black man to hate us," when in fact, the white man has never treated us right. He has never acted as a friend to us. What has he given to you and me for us to love them? Today, there is no justice in their courts for us. You are hunted like wild game throughout the country on the highways and in their towns and cities to be beaten and kill. They provoke you to have an excuse for beating and killing you. This is known all over the world and all eyes are on this treatment of the so-called American Negroes by the white man. Yet, they would like you to believe that I am the worst enemy that ever appeared among you. They do everything to keep you from believing the truth of them. They have practically one hundred percent of our black preachers following him through and under the threat of fear that they may loose their places as preachers or ministers under the white man's religious set up. They, I must repeat, under their religious set up, it was not God who set up their religion. They set it up themselves as they plainly teach you in the history of setting up of their religion, Christianity. They want you to hate truth. They want you to follow them in falsehood. They want you to remain with them though they despise you and do not like you or your color. They then come to you and say, "Elijah hates us and he teaches hatred."

I want you to remember my friend that they could have been green in color. They could have been blue colored; however, if their nature and their characteristics had been good, we would care not about their color. It could have been whatever it was made, if they were good. It would have been ok with the righteous. They would have been treated as the righteous, regardless to what color they would have been made. If they were good, we would look forward to them as a race of good people and they would be given credit and the history, but the white race doesn't have nothing in their history that teaches that they are good or ever were good, from the creation of them until this very hour of their history. Even the prophet's prophesies teaches us that they are an evil, hateful, murderous and proud people from their very beginning to their ending. They are the people that God has said, through the mouths of His prophets; that He will destroy on the day of the resurrection of the dead. They could not be a good people and have so much prophesy made in both the Bible and the Holy Qur'an about God destroying this race of people, who have build a great world and has conquered the original black people through the earth for the last 6,000 years. Now their power is draining away, and they are angry. They seek to war against the truth among you in order to prevent as many as they can from seeing the hereafter. Be aware of this.

They say to you, stay away from them. We are going to destroy them. Just like the enemies of Lot said to him in his home. They said that they would come in and destroy Lot and his guest - the Angels. But who got destroyed? It was those who declared war against Lot. We may look at Noah, who was before Lot. Who was it that got destroyed? Was it Lot or the opponents of Lot? It was the opponents of Lot. It was the opponents of Lot and the opponents of Noah who got destroyed. Who was it that got destroyed? Who destroyed in Egypt? Was it Moses or Pharaoh and his people? It was Pharaoh and His army that got destroyed who were trying to destroy Moses and his people whom God had raised up among them to lead them into a land wherein that they could be at peace.

It will be the same today. The people who know the truth, the people who know that these prophesies are on the pages of history against them, are the enemies to the truth and they seek every excuse to destroy us or bring us before their courts to condemn us as being wrong and should not believe in this teachings, because it will get them in trouble. This is another tactic of fear that they try putting into you. They target you who know that it is the truth; yet, under fear of those who fight and war against the truth that has come to you, a truth that comes to raise you up as a great nation upon this earth, you ignore the knowledge of the truth and then side in with the enemies of truth to aid them in destroying Elijah Muhammad and his followers.

Your non-acceptance of the truth, fear and great desire to befriend and be like the enemy to get what little small offerings he has, will eventually be an offense of prestige that will cause you to grieve and moan over it and finally go to hell for accepting the promises of the enemies of God and rejecting the salvation that God offered to you.

It is a shame to see how the intellectual and religious classes of our people reject and deny the truth and fight and oppose it just for the sake of being the friends of those who don't love the truth and don't want the truth. They are most surely the blind, deaf and dumb who act in such a manner.

Again, we must remember that if the white race had been made another color, green or blue, they still would have been inclined to evil, because their nature is evil and they were made in that nature and cannot help themselves; therefore, Allah is here today making them manifest to the entire world, not only to the Negroes here in America, as he's called, but to the entire world of black, brown, yellow and red people or races as they're called. Everyone is coming into the knowledge of who they are. It is prophesied that God will reveal this hidden truth of them at the end of their time. Now they are angry over this revelation that God has given to you and me and wish to impede its progress.

Anywhere there is trouble rising among the black man and his once slave master, they want to claim that Elijah's followers are the cause. They call us Black Muslims, which we don't call ourselves. We are the Nation of Islam and they would like to refer to us as the Black Moslems and have part or cause uprisings against them.

They already know that it is prophesied and

written. Moses also prophesied that the Lord thy God will vex you with an ignorant people, with a foolish people; I will vex thee. He knows who this is referring to. Its referring to the so-called American Negro. They are restless, because they want justice; restless, because God has put the restless spirit in them. He put the restless spirit in them, because they seek justice and cannot find it.

I say to you, we don't hate their color; we hate the characteristic of such a person. We hate the evil that is in them, which they cannot control. We hate their evil plans to forever deprive us of enjoying freedom, justice and equality. We hate their evil done to us in the way of beating and killing us all over the country and depriving us of equal justice with them in their court and under their law of justice. This is what we don't like about them.

They could have been any color if they had a good nature and their works were good. We would have loved them as we love our own righteous people, but nature did not give them that; therefore, we are not in love with their evil doings, nor even now do we like their color. We don't want their color, because it's a stale color; it's a color that even they don't like - pale white; nobody wants to be pale white. No one wants blue eyes; they don't like their own selves or their color, because they will do everything to sun tan themselves. It looks better than a pale white color. If God had made them under that color and put the good nature in them to do good, we would have loved them, but it is just not there.

Negro Preacher Worse Enemy to His People

Today we are having one of the worse problems ever presented to God, the world of scholars and scientist, which is resurrecting the poor so-called American Negroes, the lost and found members of our Aboriginal people of the earth - the black nation - into the knowledge of self. They have been here for the past 400 years and have lost all knowledge of self and kind; consequently, they now hate themselves and kind and cares not for uniting with his own kind, because they have fallen in love with their slave master's children. This self hatred was put into them by the slave master over the past 400 years. He was nursed into self hatred from his grandparents' and his mother's breast, while simultaneously being absolutely nursed into more ignorance and love for the slave master and his children; although they have historically proven in fact and by actual experience that they are not friends to the so-called Negroes. Yet, he's like lazarus pictured by Jesus in the Bible, still laying at the rich man's gate begging to be carried right on.

For a hundred years we have been given freedom. We have been told that we were free; yet, for a hundred years and we have become sillier today; especially you who have not the knowledge of self. The leadership have become more sillier than they were a hundred years ago, more in love with the slave master, more blind, deaf and dumber to what should be done today, which is the issue.

You don't know what to do other than to go lie down at the rich man's gate and beg him to continue bearing your responsibility throughout the years to come. You don't want to leave and go for yourself. You are too lazy for that. You don't want any responsibility for your people.

How Christianity Deceived The Black Nation

You want the white man to bear the responsibility of producing the necessities of life for us. However, Allah has come in the person of Master Fard Muhammad, to whom praise is due forever, to lead you into the knowledge of self and help you go for self, help you become independent and not a dependent ignorant people begging the white man to take responsibility caring for us, as we have for the last 400 hundred years. This is very shameful for us to be in such a condition.

The time has arrived, not to come, but is here. Judgment is now. The end of this world's white supremacy is now. It is now coming to pass. No darker people on the earth who has the freedom of doing for self or being their own ruler, wants anymore white rule over them and their people. However, on you, the Negro leadership of America, this is where the blame should be put. The political leadership of the so-called Negro and the church leadership, the preachers, who are just as frightened to say anything in defense of their people, as a mouse is to come up in the daytime before hungry cats in the house.

The Negro preacher is one of the worse enemies of his people. He's blind to the knowledge of self and hopes to keep his followers blind for the enjoyment of the slave master's children. He is their tool. He is the chief ambassador, disciple, and apostle of the slave master's children. I say to my people who are reading this book, come to some reasonable terms on what must be done for our people so that they may see, understand and live today.

Independent nations throughout the whole world are being threatened with being blown up and destroy, as Jeremiah says in his prophesy with these symbolic words: "The earth," he says, "is turned upside down and the nations are scattered abroad." I say, this can be literal, but at time, he was spiritually referring to the nations of the earth being turned upside down politically. Disagreement among them has risen to such a point of anger that they cannot reconcile themselves. They are determined to destroy each other, and you too. While all of this is going on, the leaders of the so-called American Negroes are sitting on the top of the pot lid that will blow off here in America.

America is one of the most hated people and countries of all the nations of the earth today. In fact, I should say, she is more hated than all the other countries and all the other people on earth combined. Why? Because it's the work of God; it's the work of the righteous nations. It is principally the work of the divine Supreme Being, Who has disguised himself and has come in our midst in the person of Master Fard Muhammad, to whom praises are due forever. I thank Him for coming. I thank Him for opening my eyes to the knowledge of truth and my ears and heart to understand.

The intellectual class is too proud to accept your own nation and your own God of salvation to you. You take it for fun, for absolute mockery, to be invited to join on to your own kind. You take Islam for an organization that has been created by me here in America without divine guidance, divine mercy or divine truth whatsoever. You take me for a joke. You take the truth that I preach to you as a joke. You take God Himself, Who came in the person of Master Fard Muhammad, as a joke. I fear that you are going to meet with that which Lot's people met with, who mocked him and suffered for it. Noah's people mocked him and the truth that he preached and suffered drowning in the flood of water. Moses' opponents in Egypt also suffered drowning in the Red Sea. I fear you being under the same thing as Lot's people. You are too proud. For thirty-five years I have preached to you the truth. I have defied you to disprove the truth that I have been teaching time and again. I know you're a lover of money. I have often offered you, from my follower's pocket book, $10,000 dollars to disprove what I'm teaching.

How Christianity Deceived The Black Nation

The world now believes that what I'm telling is the truth, but you are too proud to accept it, because the enemy whispers to you behind the door and tells you that you shouldn't pay it any attention. You then take it for granted that the enemy is more of a friend to you than God Himself. The Bible teaches you of this tricknology that would come upon you and the temptation of the world of evil that is now offered to you for the purpose of making you forsake your own salvation, eternal life in Allah - your God and my God - and your nation. Do you think that the Nation of Islam will be wiped from the face of the earth? If so, tell me how can they be wiped from the face of the earth, I will agree with you if you have anything. But, I know it's impossible. I know you can't do it, because the God of heaven and earth is on the side of the Muslims and against what you call Christianity.

No religion, my friends and readers, will survive this war but Islam. Islam is a religion of entire submission to the will of God Whose proper name is Allah and Who has appeared in the person of Master Fard Muhammad. You are foolish to turn it down. Islam wasn't taught to us by the white man and he can't teach it to us, because, by nature, he cannot teach you and me righteousness and you know that. You have experienced these things and you are still experiencing them today. Now what must be done with a people who willfully hears the truth and will now accept it; who willfully rejects it; who hears and knows it is the truth?

Many of the leaders of my people know it is the truth, and although our open enemies, our slave master's children, beat and kill us up and down the streets, highways and even in our places of worship, you are so in love with this people that you reject your own salvation and wish salvation from them in the way of just being allowed to work on the job, or to court, sweetheart and intermarry with them. You care not for the future of your people. You only want a future for the white race, because you have baptized yourself in love with them.

If they were beloved by God, the God of truth, freedom, justice, and equality, you would not love them more than I, but they are not the beloved of God. They are the enemies of the God of righteousness. They are the lovers of evil; they are the lovers of indecency, as you see and when you go over to them, it lets the world know this is all you care for. They are not by nature made to do righteousness and if you and me try accepting them for righteous people and righteous guides, we will be gravely mistaken. We have been gravely mistaken in this people for the last 100 years, not to think over the 300 years that they have absolutely blinded and dumbed us to the knowledge of ourselves, while beating and enslaving us all of those 300 years without any mercy whatsoever coming to us from God or our own kind. Our own kind did not know that we were here in those days; they did not know. You say, well, God always knew. Yes, but the God is prophesied as coming, not

Everything Was Going So Well, Then We Found Jesus

that He was here for you and me 400 years ago; no. It was His word that was here and the prophets were preaching the word that He would come. Now today, there is no more preaching that God will come, but God is here and I have been telling you that for thirty-five years.

I'm not preaching that God will come, but that God is present. God is with me and I am with God and I warn you that He's here presently doing just what it was predicted by the prophets He would: Gather you who believe in Him out and unite you on to Himself, your kind, and give to you a name of His own that shall live.

You make fun of His names in exchange for such names as Fish, Woods, Tree, Bush or Mr. Vine - any name that is absolutely not of the divine Supreme Being's names. You prefer names of something that doesn't refer to human beings. You like that better than you do the names or attributes of the Divine Supreme Being, which are prophesied in the book that you read every day, the Bible. It teaches you there that God would come and give you His names; yet, today you will not accept them, in the face of all of the teachings and all the proof that you hear is the truth. Even the white people themselves bear me witness in many places that this is the truth. It is you who are rejecting the truth for a favor, a good laugh, a pat on the shoulder or to be able to sit and meet with them or talk with their women. I don't blame them for kicking you out of their houses with your wanting eyes of their women. I would do the same thing to them if they came over to my house trying to look adulterously and wickedly at my women folk; I would do the same. This is the nature of people of intelligence. It is the nature of people who want a decent family. This is the nature of a people who want a decent nation. They don't want their nation spotted up. Yet, here in America, the so-called Negro leadership condones destroying his people through social integration and this wicked thing of condoning your sons to marry a white girl or your white son to marry your black daughters.

EVERYTHING WAS GOING SO WELL, THEN WE FOUND JESUS

This is one of the worse evils in the sight of Almighty God.

According to history, this took place back a long time ago. In the Bible where its says, "And the old men, ancient men," meaning the black people of the earth, "looked upon the daughters of men," meaning the white people who were grafted from the black people, that their daughters were beautiful or good to look at and they married or taken them as wives of these people. This happened in Arabia over 4,000 years ago. Their whole world is mixed with the blood of these people. There are two dominate races from the grafting of the black man to get this people to rule you and me for 6,000 years, namely the brown and yellow race.

I say my readers, my beloved people, who have been made blind, deaf and dumb, wake up before it is too late. You have only just a few hours. This is the frightful years that we are living in now. It is the frightful year of the white race on the planet earth. They are making every preparation to try remaining here. The problem now is the so called American Negro, the lost and found people of his own kind, living in the midst of this people on whom the world is now training their guns, planes, and missiles to destroy from the face of the earth, by the order of God. Finally, as the book teaches you and me, Daniel refers to it, and it's like this: "The Fourth Beast will be taken and his body given to the burning flame." This is none other than America. I want you to know the truth. This year is the frightful year of white rulership over the black people of earth. This is their year of freedom; they will loose. They will miserably loose the rule over the black man. They will do it and those who are wise among them are now trying to make preparation for safety.

They tell you what is happening. They do not deny the truth. It is you who denies the truth. They do not deny the things that they know God has made manifest. They know the truth was coming. They know the time is ripe and the truth must be preached to you. The Bible and the Holy Quran said that you must be resurrected into the knowledge of yourself. They're not trying to prevent you, but you are preventing yourself. You cannot say or accuse the white people of not letting us hear the truth. You hear it. It is nice of them to let you hear it, but they know that you are so dumb that you will never believe it and you are not believing it. I say in the strongest language I can give you, this is the year of fright.

The power of many nations of the earth will be destroyed this year. To you who owns no country, who owns no power in a country, you are helpless. You are servants of the American white people. Fly for your life; fly for your life. There must be something done about your ignorance. What should be done about your ignorance to make you or force you to come to the knowledge of God and the knowledge of yourself and your kind? I ask that question, but

I will answer: chastisement of Almighty God Allah is the only One Who can force you into submission to His will, and He forces everything of nature to bow to His will willingly or unwillingly. He also will make the American so-called Negroes bow to His will, willingly or unwillingly or be punished night and day with such grief that you cannot sleep day or night due to your regret of your ignorance or rejection. The submission to the will of Almighty God Allah has entered into His salvation for you. You won't be able to sleep nights or day.

I say, this is coming upon you, so-called American Negro, who refuses to accept Islam. What do you think Islam really is? What do you think it really is, I repeat? Islam is the true religion of God. It is entire submission to His will and if any people on earth or an individual doesn't bow in submission to the divine Supreme Being, He will not have mercy on their soul. This you should know. This you have been taught, but you don't believe. This is the time, time for what? It is the time that is the end of the white race to rule the black man on the face of the earth. This is the end of their time.

It was the end in 1914, as all religious scholars and scientists will agree that it was the end of the white man's time and God has revealed it to me that that was the end. Soon it will be fifty-two years from that time and the day have arrived. Don't look for it to be extended; it has already been extended. Grace has been given to this people. The wicked world of white mankind, for now fifty-two years, they're still just as wicked or more so today than they were in 1914. Look what you are seeing at their hands. You see blood and death as you plead to the murderer to have mercy on your soul, be easy with you, forgive you and grant you equality with the murderer and killer. You are certainly an ignorant people. And the so-called Negro leadership is absolutely the murderers and killers of their own people. I am talking about the American clergy and political classes of the so-called Negroes. They are the real murderers; for they will take you into that which has been prepared for the wicked world, death.

EVERYTHING WAS GOING SO WELL, THEN WE FOUND JESUS

GIVE UP THAT OLD SLAVERY IDEA

On the coming of Almighty God, in the person of Master Fard Muhammad, you are asked to accept your own and give up the old slavery idea of seeking heaven after you die or going to hell after you die. You must remember, as Almighty God Allah who has appeared in the person of Master Fard Muhammad, your God and Saviour and deliverer, my God and my Saviour and deliverer, has brought to you and me the real truth of heaven and hell. He has brought to you and me the real truth of God and the devil. This has been preached to you for the past 33 years. What have you to say today? What are you doing for yourself today after hearing all these truths for the past 33 years now? What can you say that you are doing for yourself or has the truth benefited you in any way? This is the answer demanded of you to give today. How have you received this truth? From your very knowledge and understanding, you know that this is the real truth, but how have you received it and how have you treated it?

I'm asking you for the answer. You cannot truthfully disapprove anything that we have given you of the truth. You cannot disprove it. You have tried all you know for the past 33 years to condemn this truth, but have you been able to do so, where is your answer? No, you have not been able to condemn it, then why haven't you then believed it since you cannot condemn it. Why have not you believed? Is it because you still desire the evil life of this world?

You still desire to go along with those who have brought you into slavery and deprived you of the knowledge of self, your kind and others. They have deprived you of the knowledge of your God and the knowledge of them as His adversary.

You have absolutely rejected this truth and have

shown the world that you refuse to recognize it and won't accept the salvation of your own, even though it is offered to you along with examples. We are an example of what God promises and has given to us. He promised you heaven: money, good friendship and good homes while you live here on the earth. However, you have rejected His true promise, which He always fulfills, to the inducement of falsehood and false promises made to you. Today, you are about to be beset on all sides; the day has arrived. The hour is approaching that when none can help the other one. No burden bearer, say's the Holy Qur'an, will bear the burden of another one. This will be the day of which the Holy Qur'an refers to as the Resurrection of the dead, around the 75th chapter (surah) of the Holy Qur'an. It teaches you there of the signs of the coming Resurrection in these words, that the very one who seeks to put his excuses upon others for his own faults will on that day accuse no one but himself of his evil and ignoring the truth. It goes something like this: "On the day when the self-accusing spirits, the self-accusing spirit - this is self accusing self of its own shortcomings and not on another" The power of Allah in the Resurrection is forcing man to accuse himself and not put his faults and blames on another one. These days are approaching. The time is at hand. Almighty God, Allah, in the person of Master Fard Muhammad, of whom the prophets prophesied, would come in person on the Resurrection Day and you shall see God in person. This has never happened before the Resurrection. The Bible and the Holy Qur'an teaches of these days and times when the evil world is ending, evil is being destroyed and the chief of evil doing and teaching will come to naught with the chief - the enemy devil who shall be destroyed and all his works destroyed. Why should not you understand? I am referring to my people. Why should not you open your blinded eyes to such clear truth? Master Fard Muhammad, to Whom be praise forever, has opened up this clear truth to you and you are rejecting it. You have rejected it for 33 years. How have you benefited from rejecting the truth, which brings you your own salvation? This is your own salvation. Why should a man rejected his own salvation for his damnation? There is no hope for you in this world with the people that have brought your fathers into slavery and seek to hold you in free slavery forever. Could you hope for salvation in such a people, answer me that? Have you got any proof in prophesy that the slave master would set free his slaves and make them his equal and provide his wealth with his slave equally or give the slave justice in their courts? Where have you found this in the past history, where a certain people have been subject to another people? Have you ever read or seen it where they were delivered and given equal justice with those who had the power to keep them as their subjects? No. Even today wherever the black man claims that he is now getting independence from the powers of the white man of Europe and America, do you not see that they are still subject? They are not completely free of the white man's power. Do not you see how West India is still is under the power of England? Great Britain exercises power and authority in West India, though they are called free people. They have their own "freedom" now; yet; there is a string tied to them.

Search the entire continent of Africa and you will see that they are fighting like mad trying to free themselves from the white man's yoke where ever they claim they have gotten freedom. Do not you see that there is still an string held by the once powers that subjected them and are yet still there under cover. They are still tied to the power of the European race and not as yet fully free. Even to Liberia, which you boast of as being you own country, she's not fully free of America. America still holds Liberia. If she wants Liberia to do any of her bidding, she has the power to do it, because she yet has a lease on Liberia. Search all the countries today that say that they have gotten their independence and see if you don't find some strings of the white man's power still there, even if it's only in the trade of vital materials that the country has to have and have to get it from the white powers as aid for that peoples' need. How many countries do you find totally free from the white man? It is hard to find; yet, here in the Western Hemisphere, you are offered heaven at once if you would submit to Almighty God Allah, in the person of Master Fard Muhammad. Think over that! He will free you indeed, as it is written in the Bible, that He will free you indeed and set you in heaven and make you an independent nation upon the planet earth as never a nation was before you. You would be made very free and happy and He will help you in every respect. He will aid you against your enemies; fight your battles for you with a very happy and delightful spirit. He delights in bringing to naught those who oppose you. He delights in destroying the enemies or the nation that will not accept you, because that nation that rejects, fight and oppose you is a nation rejecting, fighting and opposing the God, Who has accepted you and choosing you to be His people.

All kinds of opposition is now rising against you

going to your God and accepting Him as His religion and His people. Everything is now done today to make the so-called American Negroes believe that he has a happy future if he would only accept the promises of the white man, from whom there are plenty of rosy promises being made. I warn you that they won't be fulfilled.

The only promise and the only thing that they will fulfill to you is lust. They will lead you into lust. They will lead and encourage you to do everything that is opposed to your salvation, your God and your people of the righteous. They will facilitate you in every evil and filthy thing you want. The whole entire atmosphere over the country is filled with temptation and lust trying to get you to accept it and forget about a future salvation for you and your children. They are pulling off your clothes showing the nations your secret parts. You cannot hide your own secret parts from the public; for he has uncovered you and he's leading to that which no decent and intelligent nation would accept. Follow me and you will be on the right way, and the nations of the earth will respect you. Every civilized Asiatic Nation will accept you, whether they are really Muslims or not. You would be respected if you will clean up yourselves and reject the evil, filth, temptation and indecency that your slave master and their children are now offering you. They are not offering you some of this earth that you may live on in peace to yourself. They are not offering you justice in their courts; they are depriving you of that. They are taking you out and beating you all over the country. They don't want you - only for death - that's all they want you for.

They even seek to accuse us, the Muslims, in everything they think would make a charge against us of evil. They bring us before their courts to condemn us on wars. Everything that happens or all the wrongs that started in this land, they try accusing my followers and I of participating in it until it is as plain as sunshine that we are not taking part. They accuses us in every city of everything that arises there of evil, which will cause unrest and discontentment among the people. They charge it to us, but they can't use these false charges. They can't say, "Black Muslims" had a part in it. We are not "black muslims". We are the Nation of Islam. They call us black Muslims after their own naming from the press, but we are the Nation of Islam.

I want you to remember that. Refer not to us as black Muslims; we are the Nation of Islam in America. This is what we were originally known to be: The nation of Islam. Think back years ago. We were never called black Muslims, but today, they like to refer to us as black Muslims to make the world think we are a cult or something that is trying to rise up here of our own accord or that something Elijah Muhammad has manufactured and is teaching of himself, but Elijah could not have manufactured the truth that he's teaching you which the world recognize. The scientists and scholars of the world know that I'm teaching you the truth. Where did I get if from? Surely the white man did not teach me these truths; you know that. Where did he come from? He came from Almighty God Allah. I'm teaching you where we came from, but you do not believe it; yet, you cannot condemn it as being other than the truth.

My believing people and to my disbelieving people, the day has arrived that you must come to the knowledge of the truth. The day has arrived when the scripture will be fulfilled; wherein, it says that your agreement with hell will not stand. Isaiah prophesied that to you. You're trying to make an agreement with the adversaries of God between yourself and kind, that you will stick by them (white race) and will oppose Elijah Muhammad, his followers and the truth that he preach. None of you preachers have ever been able and felt like that you could win in a round table talk with Elijah Muhammad against what he's teaching; you never felt that you were strong enough to do that. That's why you never have, for 33 years, accepted an invitation by Elijah Muhammad to try and contend with him over the truth that he's teaching. You fear that you will openly be condemned and found to be absolute falsehood bearers and the ignorant teachers that you are, and inadequate to condemn the man that the country would like you to condemn. You won't be able to condemn me and the truth that I'm teaching, because it is from God. It's from Almighty Allah, Who has appeared among you and I in the person of Master Fard Muhammad. You say you can't believe in a man, but look at what your Bible prophesies would come to you in the last days. It says the Son of Man and you preach this. You preach that Jesus was God; therefore, was not he a human being? Was not he a human before and after his death? Then why are you now condemning God in the person of a man, since all that ever appeared to prophets of old were in the person of man. There never has been a time that God appeared to a man in any other form than a man, because you cannot receive anything other than yourself. You cannot receive a God claiming Himself to be something other than a human being. You would not accept anything of the kind.

Read your Bible carefully and you will find that God hears, He speaks, He knows, He walks, He talks, He sits down, and He lies down and that He is a person. Anything that is represented with the power to speak with humans, in human languages and have the power to smell, the power to hear and the power to see and the power to understand man's own affairs and have interest in the affairs of man, it must be a man. It cannot be something else. You could condemn me in trying to bring to you a God that is not man. You have no proof of this. These are only ideas or theories that cannot be supported; however, I could prove to you that God is man and is not something as immaterial as you have been made to think. You only speak on what you have been made to believe in from a child, which was that God is something other than a human being and therefore made to not even accept God in the person of a man. Who taught you this? It was the adversaries of God, the enemy of God who taught you in such a way of believing that God had no form. He did this in order to keep you blind, deaf and dumb to the knowledge of God; so, when He came to you in person, you would reject Him thinking that He's not something that is like man, though the Bible teaches you that man was made in the image and likeness of his creator. That's a man, because he could not be made in the image and likeness of a spirit that has no form.

I say to you, wake up today. The time is at hand and the hour of doom is now approaching. America is filled with nothing but evil, continuous evil, filth and indecent conduct by the nation. The atmosphere over America is filled with evil daily. The atmosphere it is filled with love songs, indecent songs, gambling and profane language that is used throughout the nation. Cursing and swearing from the cradle to the old man that is stooping upon his cane. Babies, as soon as they are taught to speak the language, are using curse words and are using all kinds of filthy language as never before since man has been on the face of the earth. I say to you, God said that He will destroy America for her evils done to His people, the so-called American Negroes.

IG WAS GOING SO WELL, THEN WE FOUND JESUS

TRUE RELIGION

The American so-called Negroes must have total separation from their slave master's children. This would be for the good of both and for a peace between the two; especially, since it has been proven that within the last 400 years they cannot live in peace together, because one is the master and the other is a slave. The master refuses to give equal justice to his slave. This problem can be successfully solved by separating the two giving his slave a proper send off. The slave master should give his slave something to go and start a life for himself, on some of this earth that he can call his own. He should give him this help until he's able to produce his own needs for about 20 or 25 years; after that, if the slave is not able and not willing to go for himself, he should either be the slave of the civilized world forever or he should be shot down by the armies of those who supported him to go for himself for the past 20 or 25 years.

In the name of Almighty God, Allah, Who appeared in the person of Master Fard Muhammad, Who brought and delivered this solution to me; total separation is His solution for the condition of peace between the slave and his master.

When referring to the religion of Abraham, we are going to use the Holy Qur'an; wherein, we will use Abraham as an example of a true believer in the true religion of Allah, which is Islam. It means entire submission to the will of Allah God. It is the only religion recognized by Almighty God according to the Holy Quran and when we understand the Bible, the religion of peace promised there to the faithful righteous on the day of judgment, it means the same as not recognizing any religion except the religion of entire submission to His will. If we will not be willing to bow to His will, there will be no such thing as safety for us.

Islam is the religion that was prophesied to be the people's religion in the hereafter. The religious worship of this world is not of God but of Satan. It is produced, financed, preached and practiced by Satan. When we understand the true meaning and significance of the word Islam, we shall all agree that nothing can be the true religion of the people in the hereafter but Islam.

In the Arabic language, Islam means entire submission to the will of God. If anyone rejects Islam or if any religious believer believes other than Islam - even an infidel, it is like saying that he or she has declared openly that they will not submit to the will of God. Today, the religion of Islam is being offered to the once lost and now found members of the Asiatic black nation in America, who are called Negroes by their slave master's children.

The word Negro means something hard, lifeless, neutral, not of this or of that. What ever you want it to do or how ever you desire to use it, you will have to tell it; for the word Negro actually means neutral, or between this and that.

This particular interpretation is not given to the so-called Negroes, because they dislike being mocked and presented to the world with such a no good and worthless name makes them out to be something they think they are not; however, it stands true that Negro means just that - something neutral, hard, and lifeless that will not do anything for self, unless it is forced by those who will make them do, then the so called Negro reacts accordingly.

He doesn't want to go from his slave master, because he doesn't know of another other people or country other than his slave master's people and country. He has been brought up and taught by his slave master; therefore, he knows nothing other than what he has been taught from his slave master and his children. He's not a member of the white race and his ways, beliefs and characteristics are not that of the original black people from whom he came; consequently, it is hard to unite the so-called American Negro on either side, because his slave masters have made him an object of hate and dislike among themselves and his own kind. He doesn't like anything that is of black or of the black nation, because he was never taught that black was original. He was never taught that the God of the universe, Who created the heavens and the earth was Black; he was never taught that. He doesn't know anything about that; he was never taught that the God Who created this world, from where this people originated and brought into being, was guided by the Black man to the road of success and put into the knowledge and power of ruling the Black race or nation for the past 6,000 years. Likewise, it is the Black man, today, who is now bestirring himself and rising up like a mighty flood to take his place again to rule his own earth and the people of the earth as he did before 6,000 years ago.

EVERYTHING WAS GOING SO WELL, THEN WE FOUND JESUS

He will have to be re-schooled, meaning the poor American Negroes will have to be re-educated into the knowledge of their own people, way of life, God and their religion, to be accepted as a brother among his own people today. The so-called Negroes have tried to imitate their slave masters and children for nearly 100 years after they were told that they were free, but has not as yet been made free indeed. He has made a very ugly mistake of it in trying to imitate their slave masters and being like them, which has disgrace him in the eyes of the civilized world of man. The slave masters have changed him so thoroughly from himself into something that they have taught them to be, which they themselves despise and hate today.

They don't recognize a so-called Negro as they recognize themselves as equal in civilized society. They don't like being classified with a Negro in society, because they teach their children that a Negro is nothing. Their children are taught from the cradle to hate, despise and look down on the Negro as something which is not equal as they are and not even human or equal. They don't see a Negro as being equal to a human. They even classified him according to history in slavery as being 3/5ths of a human being and this has brought the Negro into a very low state of respect among the civilized people of earth.

The slave master demands someone to prove to him or them that the so-called Negro is not their own property. This is why the Bible prophesies that we must be redeemed and a redemptive price must be paid for the freedom of the lost and found members of the Asiatic Black Nation, because the slave owners claim us to be their property and will do everything they possibly can to prevent them from returning to their own people, God and religion, which is Islam.

This work of deception is going on today. The great work of the Christians to tempt and deceive our people is under way full blast and will probably capture 90 percent of the black people of America, which is not an invitation to do righteousness; but in fact, an invitation to hellish behavior, evil doing and indecency. The entire atmosphere over North America is now filled with evil, filth and indecent practices right before our eyes over the radio, television and now the internet. We see and hear the evil, filthy songs and dances that are so filthy that even dogs, if they understood how to do such filthy dances, would be ashamed to do it in the eyes of civilized people.

The churches are not protesting these evil and filthy practices among the people; therefore, the churches and the preachers of what is called the gospel of Jesus are guilty of being sympathizers with such evil and filth. They are not protesting against this disgrace within their own religion called Christianity, which publicly displays every evil and filth act in the ears and the eyes of everyone in America and throughout the civilized world of man. The church falls short of this and is found guilty before God today for being a friend and sympathizer of the devil and his evil, indecent, and temptation now practiced on God's people of righteous. The church permits evil and indecency to come in and become part of their worship. This takes the form of indecently dressed women, who make up the congregation of the church. The church and its services are sometimes carried out in the tone of other than divine. All of this is going on in the eyes of the civilized world of man with the common Christians and church leaders backing it up. This makes it clear to the eyes of the world that Christians and those who preach Christianity, the doctrine of Christianity, are the worst divine law breakers of all people, because the most ugly, evil and filthiest things are practiced in the church! This is why I take up the subject of true religion, to which you have failed to submit.

The author of the true religion is the True God. Islam, the true religion of God and His prophets was brought and taught you, but we received persecution, disgrace, mockery and murder at your hands for teaching you the true religion. The Christian race claims that they are the light bearers of truth of the true religion of Jesus and his Father, who is the God of heaven and earth, but in deed they rejected and persecuted the believers of the true religion of Jesus, which you know as will as I was Islam. It was the religion of Abraham, Isaac, Jacob and the Scribes.

With this corruption going on in the church and being preached on the air filling the air waves with this "glorious worship," while claiming that a God in the skies or one whom they call a mystery spirit somewhere is sitting down taking note on visible human beings and having a role or record to present to them on the judgement day, which is untrue, they teach this to the public and at the same time claim themselves to be pure believers in the God of truth. How could they claim this, while at the same time permitting filthy practices to go on at the very hour of their sermons and service without protest?

If the church and it's leaders would unite against the evil and against the filthy practices in the public or in secret, especially in the presents of their children, whom they now cannot control, teach or lead rightly, it would be better for them. In the schools, colleges and universities of the land, filthy practices are being performed even by the children from 5 years old on up to one hundred years old. All of this is in the eyes of the "divine" so-called preachers, priests and leaders of the church without any uniting against it protesting. It too is practiced in the government which is called Christianity. This government is set to be based upon the Christian religion and it allows all of this to go on, from gambling to murder. Injustice is the order of the day and the practice and doing of filth and indecency; yet, the church claims that it is the divine way to God and is the way of the prophets and the house of the very son of God. I say you should repent; you should clean yourself up. You should protest evil if you are holy and sanctified, then you should unite together and see that your government does not permit evil and filthy practices in public, not to mention giving them a license to do these things. In your presence and among your members, these evil practices are now sitting on in your church and they are looking at you and you know they are there; yet, you are not able to convert them from evil to righteousness.

I say to the leaders of the church, it is time that you yourselves prove that you have a true religion and that you are worshiping the true God that made the heavens and the earth and follow the guidance of His prophets; it is time. You have shown yourself to be the friends of this evil world. You have again twisted and mixed the original truth of the scriptures of the prophets with falsehood and have labeled it with the good name of Jesus to make the people believe and swallow so they may think that they are following the true religion of God through Jesus Christ; when in reality and in deed, you know that you they not. The birth place your own religion called Christianity is after Jesus' death and not before, nor did Jesus teach it. He's not the author of it. How can you call it the religion of Jesus when the founder did not teach it in his lifetime? <u>Jesus could not be the author of Christianity</u>, <u>because the history proves that he could not.</u> <u>He did not teach it himself while he lived</u>.

Take a look at the 2 chapter and 131 verse of the Holy Qur'an; wherein it states, *"And who forsakes the religion of Abraham but he who makes a fool of himself?"* Let us take a look at the condition of the world today. There is nothing in this world but confusion, anger of the nations against each other, and ruler against ruler. Everywhere we get news is evil and anger against one another. Every government is at discord with the other one or is at war almost against each other and some are at war. The world is in a terrible condition, although the cause is from those who represent themselves as the true guides and representatives of God and His son Jesus; what a world, what a world. The nations and God is angry against the evil nations.

Confusion seems to result with every attempt to bring about peace. You cannot do it, because you refuse to submit to the author of peace. The true God and His true religion are rejected and mocked by you. Rejection of the true religion classifies you, by the wise, among the foolish.

You boast of Abraham and claim that you believe he was a true prophet. Both the Jews and the Christians claim him to be their prophet. Abraham was not of the Jewish religion or of the Christian religion. Abraham lived before Moses, the Torah and the Injil, which Jesus brought; therefore, how could you represent him as being your leader or your guide in religion when he did not even live before a scripture was even given to you? Moses gave you the first scripture. There was no scripture given to the Caucasian race before Moses. How can you say now that Abraham is your prophet or that you recognize his religion when you do not even recognize the religion that was given to you by Moses and the prophets after him? You don't recognize Jesus' religion, which was the religion of Moses, Abraham and Noah. Therefore, the Jews and the Christians cannot claim him to be the founder of their religion. Abraham was not a Jew. Abraham was an Arab. He was of the darker people, not of the Caucasian race. Ishmael and his mother Haggar were also of the darker people. This is true according to the true history of Abraham and his people as mentioned in the Holy Quran. Abraham was and Arab. His travel and worship was in Arabia and he visited the Holy City, Mecca, where all of us today who are Muslims go and pay respects and honor to that prophet and his son Ishmael and his mother Haggar. The Black Stone is a sign, which Abraham set up as a sign of the lost and found members of the great Asiatic Nation; namely the now found members of Abraham's religion and nation.

EVERYTHING WAS GOING SO WELL, THEN WE FOUND JESUS

ACCEPT YOUR OWN AND BE YOURSELF

You are acting very foolish, because you don't understand who you are or anyone else. I thank Almighty God, Allah, in the person of Master Fard Muhammad for coming and teaching me and others the knowledge of self and the knowledge of those other than ourselves. I thank Him for such great wisdom and salvation, which he has brought to us. I think you should also join me in being happy for the great salvation that has come to us, which we thought would only come after we were dead in the grave. Yet, today we now know that it will not be after a physical death, but after a mental death of us. After we had lost the knowledge of ourselves, our kind, others, the knowledge of God and His true religion, then God Himself would come to teach us the knowledge of self and restore us again into that which is our own.

EVERYTHING WAS GOING SO WELL, THEN WE FOUND JESUS

For now 35 years I have been teaching you that which Almighty God, Allah, in the person of Master Fard Muhammad, to whom praises be forever, has taught me and gave to me to give to you. He gave us His words, as it was written of Him. If you did not accept it, He said that He would destroy you along with the wicked that destroyed you mentally. Seeing that you are very ignorant and very hard to get to believe in the truth of your own self, I have chosen this subject again and again of his wisdom: Accept Your Own And Be Yourself.

The doors of the white man have been open to you for you to integrate and intermarry with him. This is something you should be suspicious of, because in the past, the white man would actually shoot you down outright for even trying to get into his family with your black self. He has lynched thousands of our people and even burned them at stake in the South, as you will bear me witness, for making any such attempt to mix blood with he and his family.

Yet, today you seem to have forgotten all of these evil things done to you just yesterday concerning mixing with this people. They all are not ready yet to agree with the government to allow you to mix with their family.

You must remember that your Bible warns you of this intermixing, which it states is designed to deceive you. You have been reading the Bible all of your lives, listening to it being preached; so, I'm not saying anything you have not heard or anything you have probably have not read in the Bible that verifies the truth of what I'm saying. You have not learned the true knowledge of God. You have been blinded into thinking that He is some kind of a spook or some formless thing that has no form at all or that He's just a voice in space or a voice to messengers, prophets and apostles; but no. Today you must know, as the Bible predicted, that God would come. The Holy Qur'an said; "Allah will come." You must remember that if the books are predicting that God would come, then that God is not already here. He would have to come. I'm referring to yesterday up to 6,000 years ago, when we have been reading and hearing that He was prophesied to come. However, today, I preach to you that He's here in your midst, but He came as it was written of him - without observation. This is true. They didn't know Him, but them to whom He revealed Himself, they became the son's of God.

I want you to know that this coming had not passed; it did not come to pass in the past histories of the prophets. It did not come to pass in Jesus time; for they killed he and his followers. It was a prediction for the last days. "Behold, He will come; the Son of Man will come, and all the Angels with Him. It is written like that in your book. The Son of Man means a son of another man, not a spirit as you have been made to believe. You have not had enough scriptural teaching and especially the truth of the scripture taught to you. You have looked for this truth to come from those who blinded you to the knowledge of truth, and not only was this truth not to come from them, it was not to come until the end of their time. Your Bible teaches you this in II Thessalonians, that God would come after the workings of Satan, and in many other places you are taught that God would come at the end of the world, as Jesus prophesied. The end of the world here means the end of the present world today as you know it - the white man's world and this race of people. This is what the Bible teaches concerning the world coming to an end. It means the white man's world; this is well known by him. He has always known the truth of what will come upon his civilization. He's not blind to that today. He's not out here arguing with me about the truth of what I'm teaching. He knows that I am teaching the truth, because he understands it himself. It's in his Bible that he gave to you after keeping you blind, deaf and dumb to the knowledge of it when he held you and your fathers in servitude slavery; this is known.

EVERYTHING WAS GOING SO WELL, THEN WE FOUND JESUS

These are facts that you cannot deny, but you do so, because you don't want to believe in the facts. What's so wrong with your own that you do not want to accept it? Is it because of they have blinded you so thoroughly that you now hate yourself and when I teach you the truth of the white man you say that now I am teaching hate. You feel this way, because you love the white man and want to be his color and intermarry with them. Now that you are learning that God has declared them to be a race of devils, you don't like this, because you want them to be your wives and your sweethearts and husbands. Yet, I must tell you the truth. It is time that the truth be told. God is backing me up to tell you the truth and the world of the righteous is backing me up to tell you the truth and if the world of the righteous doesn't back me up, God is sufficient. Allah is well sufficient to back me up to teach that which He bids me to teach and if I don't teach the truth He gave me to give to you – for the purpose of saving you from the destruction that is now coming upon this world - then I also will be destroyed and I don't want to make no such attempt to run from this truth as Jonah made. He yet had to suffer being cast overboard and had to go and do the mission that he was bid to do anyway. God never changes His word. When He chooses a man to do a thing, He doesn't like to change His mind saying, "I made a mistake by choosing Jonah; I'm going to send John or James in his place, because he ran from me." God doesn't do no such thing as that. He already knew Jonah and what he was going to do; as He's a foreknowing God when He chooses a messenger to deliver a message to a people. He knew the future of that messenger. He knew everything about him. He knows what will happen and how He prepared to take care of whatever happened and the messenger. He had already prepared in Himself what He will do, but He doesn't change the choice of the man at all. There is no such thing as another being chosen to go in that one's place; no sir. The man that God chooses to deliver a message to a people or nation is never changed and you can't change that man for another one even yourself. You have to accept that same man as the Israelites had to accept Moses; regardless to their criticism of him. The people had to accept Jesus regardless of their criticism and mockery of him. They still had to accept him. Regardless to whatever you charge a messenger with, whether it be evil, filth or whatever you may charge him with, that doesn't make God charge him with that. It doesn't make God fire him or send him into exile, because God already knew the messenger that He chose. He knows his life when He chose that man; therefore, the wicked, disbelievers, and the hypocrites will always teach that such men are not the chosen of God.

Read the history of all the prophets of God, you will find the same old story of the hypocrites and the disbelievers. They all simply just disbelieved in the man who was given to them and charged him with being a liar. They all tend to say these things and act this way. We don't pay attention to what people might say; we know that they will say these things, but what we are paying attention to is delivery of the word. Our objective is to deliver the message of God, which has been delivered to us. You will find that all those messengers wanted to do was to get over the message to the people, and as far as the people believing in their doom or accepting it as a warning from God, that was entirely up to them. The messenger delivered that message regardless of whether they accept it or reject it.

This message is being delivered to the American so-called Negroes today. Their time has come, as the Bible prophesies in Revelation around the 11th chapter and 18th verse, that the nations were angry and God was angry. It is the time of the dead and the time of warning the dead. Why is this lost and found member of the Aboriginal people – who is not a Negro - called dead by the prophets? He is mentally dead and not physically dead. He's mentally dead to the knowledge of self, the knowledge of the truth, the knowledge of God, the knowledge of his salvation and the knowledge of the adversary of

EVERYTHING WAS GOING SO WELL, THEN WE FOUND JESUS

God - the devil. If you read these chapters that bear me witness, which state that the time is here, I think you will be doing yourself a favor if you then believe these truths of the Bible's prophets predictions of this time that we are living in.

God comes, according to II Thessalonians; around the fourth verse there you will find it, after the workings of Satan. God would come after the man of sin's works have manifested to you a history of yourself and your fathers under his fathers as slaves and how he treated your and my fathers under the lash and unto death. His works would reveal how he killed them out right; right before the eyes of his guests for no more than improperly dancing or singing some songs that he wanted them to sing.

Our parents were actually treated so evil that it would not be equal we were to give the white man the same treatment. God wouldn't even give him what he gave to us; therefore, God just decided to just burn him up and get rid of him. This is written your Bible and Holy Quran. Should not you know these things? Should not you be happy that God fulfilled His prophesy, that He would raise one of you up into the knowledge of all these hidden truths or misunderstood truths? Should you not be happy that God gave it to you so that you would understand it?

The Bible goes so far as to teach us that it would be made so plain by the Warner and teacher of the truth in the last days, that a fool could not error in understanding. I, not being a college or university graduate of this people's institutions of education, cannot make it so that you would not understand, because I don't speak those old big words. Pardon me, I don't mean to criticize the words by saying old, they are words used to shorten many words, which an educated person would use to get over what he is trying to say to the people. It then would take that type of people or such an educated people to understand a man like that. Therefore, if the man is going to speak generally, he must speak a language that all the people who listens can understand. I can't speak anything other than plain language; so, don't laugh at me if by chance you have knowledge of better language. You are welcome to take the truth and the words that God has given to me for you, put it into a better language - as long as you do not destroy the meanings of what I have said in my little simple way of getting it over to you.

Don't be proud just because you have learned your slave master and his children's language better than others of your kind, but be happy that you have learned and be happy that you can be able to help the simple ones among you, not in a way of mockery. This is wrong for you to do that. You will fall into the category of the proud. It is prophesied in your book that God comes to destroy proud people. He doesn't love proud them. He punishes the proud. So be not one of them.

He asks you and me to accept our own today and then tells us what our own is. We are of the righteous and He forgives us for the sins committed under the rule and guidance of the Caucasian race, the white man, the enemy of truth and righteousness. He forgives us of that. The white man brought us and our fathers here 400 years ago and made us other than ourselves. As a result of his misguidance, he mislead us against Almighty God, whose proper name is Allah. He misled us in the knowledge of Him who was coming to save and deliver us. Those of us who believe in that One and who believes in the last day, he deceived us in such way that we always mistook God to be something that he really was not. Such charges against us, he said, He will not even remember. He said these same words to me that you read there in the Bible, that He would not even remember our sins and will not bring them to us or charge us with them.

As you noticed, the Bible teaches that all the dead would be saved if they only believed. Again it teaches that all the dead would rise, as Jesus prophesied of it in a symbolic way there in the Bible. You have it that the day will come that all who are in the grave shall hear his voice and come forth. You have taken it literally just like it reads there, which it did not mean. It doesn't mean that dead bones in the earth or some in the grave that doesn't have no sign of the bones there is coming back to earth. This is not what this prophesy was referring to; it wasn't referring to that at all. It meant that a people who are mentally dead would rise up in the judgment or the resurrection. It's referred to in name as a rising up of a people into a higher knowledge of divine and this people would be raised up to teach their people a higher knowledge of God and His wisdom. God would chose them to become His beloved people and He would put them on top of civilization or on top of the world of man; thus making them a people greater than any that ever was since man had been on the face of the earth. This God's wisdom, according to the prophets, is supreme to any other's wisdom that ever was. He has Supreme Wisdom and there is no relation to His wisdom. He can make a people who has no limit to their future and there is none who could compete with His people and His wisdom.

He brings the wisdom of the wise of this world and those before these people and reduces it into nothing. In comparison to what He brings, what they have is something He could laugh at, because of His great unmatched wisdom of anyone here today or anyone that will come in the future. You mean to say that you don't want your own to be a part of that? No sir, you are wrong; you are acting like a fool. You don't want to accept such a God Who wants to exalt you with His great wisdom above all the nations of the earth that ever was? I think you should run to such a God. He wants to give you His own name; He offers that name to you. He's given it to us who believe and accept Him as our God and have accepted the truth brought to us, which is the true religion of God, entire submission to His will, called Islam by the Arabs in the Arabic language.

I want you to know that Master Fard Muhammad has taught us in accord with what the prophets taught that God would teach on His coming and that at the end of the world, He would make manifest the enemy who has deceived and ruled the people by teaching them other than the truth. However, God will come to reveal the enemy of truth as an enemy of truth and not a truth bearer or lover of truth, because he wasn't made not such.

Today you have read this, now I want you to remember that if you love yourself and your kind, accept your own self, accept your own kind. What's wrong with it? You have always been taught that black is original haven't you? Certainly you have. You don't find in the chemistry world that they take black out of white. Why should you think then that the white race are the first people of the earth, God's chosen and beloved people, when you have by experience known that you cannot take black out of white. If there was any color like white made, it would have had to come from black and not from itself, because white was not the producer of the first people. We have a history of them, as God taught us; their number is 6,000 years on our planet, but we have no birth record.

Accept your own and be yourself. You don't want to submit to God? That's what Islam means. You don't want to be one of God's people when He's telling you that you're one of them? You don't want to have Him forgive you of your sins? You don't want to see the hereafter, where God and the darker people live? The whole earth belongs to that people and you're invited to take your place with them.

Accept it or you may reject it; that's up to you, as I say, As Salaam Alaikum.

Thank you for purchasing this book. We trust the reading was rewarding and enlightening.

We offer various titles and a comprehensive collection of Messenger Elijah Muhammad's works. These works include:

- Standard Published Titles
- Unpublished & Diligently Transcribed Compilations
- Audio Cassettes
- Video Cassettes
- Audio CD's
- DVD's
- Rare Articles
- Year Books
- Annual Brochures

You are welcomed to sample a listing of these items by simply requesting a FREE archive Catalog.

Our contact information is as follows:

Secretarius MEMPS Ministries
12685 Dorsett Rd. #187
Maryland Heights, Missouri 63043
Phone and Fax 314.564.4003
secmm@sbcglobal.net - Web: www.memps.com

Wholesale options are also available.

Made in the USA